The Best Little Things

The Best *Little* Things

The Little Lessons That Life Brings Our Way and How They Can Make a Big Difference

By
Morgan Wolf

The Best Little Things

The Little Lessons In Life That
Can Make a Big Difference

Published by: Morgan Wolf
Editorial and Print Layout: Jim Rogers
Illustrations by: Ian Hanna
Cover Design: Morgan Wolf, Jim Rogers
Cover Image: Brandon Wolf

For my mother who taught me to
"go forth and conquer."
And for my husband, Brandon, who has presented
me with so many of the best little things ever…
and for everyone who's ready to upgrade their own mindset.

Why read this book?

What could you gain if you did?

First of all, in reading this book, you should definitely get more than a few laughs... and hopefully learn a few things along the way. This book is a collection of stories and lessons from my life and the people I share it with.

Contents

Foreword

Life is filled with lessons. During those times of reflecting on our past, most of us tend to recall the big lessons of life and wonder why it took us so long to learn them. (Among those lessons are: say you're sorry, cherish the people you love, value what's important to you and not others, and so on.) However, this book is not about the big lessons in life – not about realizing that I initially invested myself in the wrong career for me, or that I shouldn't have moved to another city when I did, or not even about the 'one that got away'.

Instead, it's from my own life experiences (and the many lessons that I've learned along the way), that I've come to understand that it's not the big lessons in life that matter most of all, but the smallest lessons that are presented to us each and every day that make the biggest difference.

It's these small lessons – when we take the time to see them, internalize them, and apply them to our lives – that become 'the best little things' in our lives.

The focus of this book is the concept of mindset and how it affects our daily life, moment by moment.

It's the proper mindset that allows us to see these lessons in the first place. Without a 'responsible mindset' you'll never see them, and worse yet, you'll only complain about them. In doing so, you'll choose a victim mentality and blame someone else for your misery. However, the misery that you experience is simply the result of your mindset... or the way that you choose to view those 'best little things' (or the lessons) that are presented to you every single day. If you are the victim of life and other people's actions, then you're not the one in control of your life. Therefore you're not able to create the changes that you seek. If you operate from a place of responsibility and choose to take the action towards what you want your life to look like, then you take back the control to make the life of your dreams.

> *"Dance as though no one is watching you, love as though you have never been hurt before, sing as though no one can hear you, live as though heaven is on earth."*
>
> - Audrey Hepburn

Whether those lessons have to do with the friends that you've held onto for too long, for failing to treat yourself with the same respect that you give others, or for realizing that the differing views of those people you love are necessary for you to grow and flourish, all of these 'best little things' often started out as those things to complain about as opposed to being things that you can grow from as a result of them coming your way.

Learning about the fact that 'life is about attitude and the good news is that I get to choose it', has been a game-changer for me.

While on its own, nothing in this book is earth-shattering, when you put everything together, it can become a very powerful, life-changing force for you.

At the end of each chapter is an exercise I've included that will help you internalize these lessons for your own self-awareness. Many people do not like to write in a book, if this is you, I suggest a separate notebook for the exercises. Otherwise, space has been provided for you to complete them in the book. If it helps, you can think of this more as a workbook than one that just sits on your bookshelf when you're done reading it. No matter what your style, I strongly encourage you to take some time for your self-growth and complete each exercise.

You can either passively read this book for entertainment, or actively read it by doing the exercises. If you choose to participate, you can benefit from these lessons in your daily life. As a result of your work, you'll begin to realize the many fruits of your labors.

This is why I wrote this book... as an entertaining teaching tool to pass on the things that I've learned, often via 'the hard way', to save you some of the pain of discovery that learning lessons 'the hard way' can bring to you. If I've done that with this book, then I've achieved my goal. My hope is to help you achieve yours too!

Introduction

Plain and simple, this book is about mindset. It's not a book about goal setting, or 'ten steps' to fix your life. (In fact, I'm not here to tell you – or anyone else for that matter – that you need to fix or change something in your life.) Instead, it's about the way that you look at the world and how such a mindset affects the outcomes that you experience.

What I will say about this book is this: if you don't like the results that you've been getting in one or more areas of your life, then perhaps you may consider the tools that I have to share with you here. These are tools that I've learned myself; tools that have produced positive results in my own life, and tools that will help you create a set of similar results that you would like to see in your own life. Better yet, they have the power to help you do so with a reasonable amount of speed and efficiency.

My view (and I have a lot of subjective evidence to support it) is that I have the life that I have because I've chosen it. While I didn't choose the hand that I was dealt, I do get to choose how I play the cards; the good, the bad, the great... and the awful.

I choose the way that I respond to everything that happens to me, along with the space or value that I give it in my life. Anything and everything that I experience gets filtered through the lens of the way in which I view the world. If I don't like the first reaction that comes to mind, then I have the power to search for a different option. It has taken a lot of practice for me to learn how to first breathe, then take the all-important moment that I need to respond to a situation in the way that aligns with who I truly want to be.

"Knowing yourself is the beginning of all wisdom."
- Aristotle

I recently re-read Seven Habits of Highly Effective People by Stephen Covey. In it he reminded me that you never truly master something. The better I get, and the more time I invest in whatever I choose to work on in myself, the more I realize that I still have more to learn. Once I get to a 'ten out of ten', I start over because I've leveled-up that skill.

As an example, if someone doesn't know anything about math and then they learn about addition and subtraction, they can then master those basic principles. Once they've mastered addition and subtraction, then they're ready to learn about division and multiplication, and so on. Then once they've figured all of that out, they throw in letters (you know, those nasty 'variables') with everything and they have to start with the basics all over again.

Learning is a progressive experience, which builds on the knowledge that you've already learned.

Let me preface the following by saying this: no person

should steal, cheat, lie, or harm another simply to get their way. Beyond that, the world is a game, and one that we are all playing. With that said, realize that while there are no 'hard and fast' rules with respect to how you play, there are very real consequences for any and all of your actions.

> *"Let me be clear about this: I don't have a drug problem, I have a police problem."*
> - Keith Richards

For a famous rockstar, drugs were not a problem – whether getting them, using them, or working while on them – only the consequences were a problem… if he was caught by the authorities.

It's my belief that if you aren't hurting anyone or impeding their freedoms to live their life in the way they choose (i.e., one can afford and maintain their life without cheating, stealing, or harming others), then I don't have a problem with you or your actions.

My life is amazing because I say so. Well… more accurately, because I think so! To say the least, I am incredibly grateful for what I have. I work hard – I set and achieve new (and often fun) goals in my personal and professional life. I am also constantly willing to learn and make choices that bring me closer to my idea of a perfect life. There are plenty of projects that I enjoy that would be a chore or absolute punishment for others. There are definitely two sides to this coin because there are also plenty of things that other people enjoy that I could not be paid enough to do. In short, happiness is in the eye of the beholder.

My opinion about my life is the only one that really matters.

Your opinion about your life is the only one that really matters.

I have a home and people to share it with. I am, by my own definition, a good person who relishes in creating joy and love in the world. I have much more fun making other people smile than sharing my frustrations or shortcomings with anyone.

However, while I feel that my life is good (in fact, way more than just 'good'), the life that I live is one that I have chosen for myself. It's taken a lot of work for me to get where I am. All I have to say is this: If I can do this, so can you.

The **most important take away** of this book is this:

Getting to know yourself is one of the best ways that you can spend your time.

"He who knows others is learned;
he who knows himself is wise."

\- Lao-Tzu

EXERCISE:

Take a moment to write a few 'I am' statements that you are proud of or working towards realizing in your own life: (Don't overthink it!) A few examples to help you with this are the following:

- I am successful.
- I am confident.
- I am powerful.
- I am strong.
- I am getting better and better every day.
- All I need is within me now.
- I wake up motivated.

1.
2.
3.
4.
5.

Now read them out loud. Now that you've done this, read them again... and then a third time just for good measure.

<u>Say</u> them, <u>think</u> them, and <u>feel</u> them daily. In doing so, you will notice that you recognize when you are embodying these traits throughout the day.

Things You Should Know About Me...

My husband's name is Brandon; he's AMAZING! We have 4 cats, 2 goldfish, and a dog.

I AM HILARIOUS, however, not everyone gets that about me... but it's true! I mean, if you lived in my head, you'd think so too.

With all that said, I can also be sarcastic, unintentionally rude, and a bit loud. Yet, on the other hand, I can also be incredibly kind, caring, and loving.

I also happen to be a wild one with a heart of gold. One of my favorite things to do is help people. However, it's because of this trait I've found a real problem, at least for me:

Not everyone wants, or is ready for, help... at least not in an obvious way.

While it can be easy to see when someone needs you to lend a hand by opening a door or taking a bag, it's not always as easy when someone needs you to lend an ear or open your heart.

At times I curse or swear, and at times in a rather loud and brash sort of way. Why? I've come to learn that I do this because I am passionate, but unfiltered. One important lesson that I've learned about myself is that my style is not for everyone. For those of you who can relate, I desire to give you some words of wisdom, share some of the other lessons that I've learned, and help you gain a deeper understanding of your own true self.

Chapter 1

Put Yourself on the List

This is a pretty simple concept and yet I still struggle with it. Even as I'm writing this book, I am having to practice this principle in order to continue to fully ingrain it in my subconscious and in doing so manifest it in my daily life.

"No one can make you feel inferior without your consent."
- Eleanor Roosevelt

If you feel like you haven't been a priority in your life, then it's time to look at how you are letting that happen, otherwise, it will never change. If you don't put yourself on the list, you can't expect anyone else to do so either... or at least, not for long.

I have found that life is a journey of both learning and experience. Sometimes, if you're lucky, you can even learn lessons from other peoples' experiences. Learning, and being open to learning, is one of the most important aspects of life!

However, I have also found that simply knowing something doesn't mean that I will actually put it into use or action. I can even have a thorough understanding of how something works, but if my experience is that I don't care, then there is no motivation for me to take action. However, if my experience is that I enjoy or connect with something, then for me action comes naturally.

When I have actually learned from an experience, instead of just gaining the intellectual knowledge, I am much more likely to adopt the principle that was presented to me. When I was a kid and someone said, "Don't touch that it's hot!" and I did it anyway, the experience of burning my hand was definitely a stronger motivator than the grown up telling me, "It's hot." Fully connecting your knowledge with your experiences is the key to making lasting changes in your life.

One of my favorite jobs was one where I was the "Shop Mom" to a group of about ten guys. While on paper I was the "Operations Manager," in reality it was the 'anything' role, meaning that it entailed doing 'whatever was necessary to keep everyone happy, fed, and doing their job. Well, while we all know that you can't control someone else's happiness, I sure did try!

Every day the company bought lunch for everyone (whether they were staff or sub-contractors) and anyone who was going to be there at lunchtime. It was just that type of workplace, which was a big part of why I loved working there. Due to my role there, part of my job was ordering lunch for everyone every day.

While it was pretty straight forward, it wasn't always simple. There were days that I would plan an order from somewhere that had been shut down. Then there were other days when the food that had been delivered was all wrong and nothing was labeled. Then at other times, meals were either getting combined or delivered in an absolutely soggy condition. I could not believe all the ways that a lunch could go wrong! Then when you added my human imperfections into the situation, there were times when I either ordered from the wrong location or I forgot someone altogether.

While I learned so many lessons about placing large group food orders every day, none of those are the reason for this story.

Before going any further with this story, I would like to clarify a bit about two words that we seem to use interchangeably in our conversations: simple and easy. These are not interchangeable terms. Something can be simple, but not easy. For example, a simple set of steps on a list may be the following:

1) Pressure wash the entire 25 by 30 foot barn.
2) Apply the base coat primer.
3) Paint the barn.

While the list may be as simple as one, two, three, none of those steps are in the least bit easy to carry out. Not to mention the fact that they are incredibly time consuming and without the right tools, such a 'simple task' could turn into a disaster. I hope that I made myself clear on the difference between simple and easy. Now back to my point.

I would take orders for lunch each day, writing them on a scrap piece of paper that I found lying around my desk. Most days I would organize them by whatever method I wanted to for that day... either by department one day, or alphabetically on another. Yet if someone was being an ass to me, they would definitely be at the bottom of the list, no matter how I'd written it. However, no matter how I'd organized it, I had an incredibly difficult time putting myself on that list. In fact, I would often end up at the bottom of my scribbled notes as an afterthought. My justification was that I knew what I wanted to order, so I didn't really need to put it down.

But that was a lie.

Deep down I knew that one of my toughest adversaries was self-doubt... not feeling worthy or deserving of things. In order for me to achieve greater results in my life, my self-esteem has been the most important thing for me to work on.

While it's easy to say that you 'love yourself', it is a very different thing for you to mean it. I'm talking about the kind of love for yourself that you can really and truly feel deep down in your soul... the kind of love for yourself that you can say out loud and not feel awkward about saying the words, "I LOVE ME!" It's the 'keep the commitments that you make to yourself' kind of love... or the kind of love that allows you to look in the mirror and fully love yourself with no reservations. No judgment of imperfections is needed, nor is it helpful. When you look at yourself, you both know and accept why things are the way that they are, and if there is something that you're working on, you can love yourself during that part of the journey... or any part for that matter.

So, my self-worth boiled down to a list on a scrap piece of paper... and I couldn't even be at the top of that list. How was I ever going to achieve my goals and dreams if I couldn't even put myself first for something as simple as lunch?

After having this revelation, I did really well at putting myself on the list... and I wasn't even at the bottom!

In fact, I put myself right in the middle, just like I ranked myself in life. Why? The middle was easy. It was a place where I wasn't miserable; a place where I could have some stuff, but didn't do so much that I risked losing much of anything. Then one day I challenged myself to just put me at the top of that list... no matter what, just start with my name.

I could not believe how difficult this was for me to do!! Day, after day, after day, after day, I struggled to do this one simple thing. It was a daily sign to my subconscious that I didn't value myself and was unwilling to put my wants or needs ahead of anyone else.

I hate to admit how long I let this go on.

So, I won't.

> *"You yourself, as much as anybody in the entire universe, deserve your love and affection."*
> - Buddha

It took a lot of soul searching to bring forth what was necessary to change the feeling behind the behavior. Once I had a burning desire to be great, to be first in my own mind and to see what the top felt like, the behavior changed on its own.

With this inner realization, I finally put myself at the top of the list... consistently and without question. As a result, I felt a real sense of accomplishment because it was a small step on my long journey of self-mastery.

No one else on the team saw this list or even cared about it one bit. And yet telling myself that "I'm first" took more than a year for me to do.

I found that repetition was the key. I had to put myself first every day in order to keep up the momentum.

Repetition after repetition, I started to gain momentum and build towards a confidence that would finally come from within.

If you learn something that you want to adopt into your life, you need to connect with it, understand how it will benefit you to have it, then identify what will you have to give up in order to get it.

Scenario 1

Goal: Get up at 5:30am and workout for an hour.

Motivation: Be in better shape.

Knowledge and Tools: I know lots of fitness routines. I have worksheets, rep lists, videos, playlists, workout clothes, sneakers, arm band phone holder, headphones, water bottle, and pre-workout drink.

Outcome: No change.

Scenario 2

Goal: Get up at 5:30am and workout for an hour.

Motivation: Being fit allows me to play with my dog and go on rides with my husband.

Knowledge and Tools: I know lots of fitness routines. I have worksheets, rep lists, videos, playlists, workout clothes, sneakers, arm band phone holder, headphones, water bottle, and pre-workout drink.

Outcome: A commitment to my fitness that manifests itself naturally by working out and making healthy eating choices. Eating right wasn't even part of my goal but it is a happy biproduct of finding inspiration vs. motivating yourself to do something.

Sometimes it is just a matter of shifting your mindset and being more in touch with your true reason for achieving the goal.

For instance, if you want financial freedom and you currently live an expensive lifestyle, you will have to realize a greater income to have the freedom to maintain that lifestyle. However, if deep down within you want to live in a tiny home and travel, move to a condo in the city of your dreams, or build your own cabin in the woods, then your goal of financial freedom becomes dramatically different.

With scenario two, I do find myself changing what the workout looks like to better fit my goal. The motivation creates a desire that cultivates that creativity. In this, realize that it's important to be flexible about how you get to your goals. Allow me to explain by example.

If fitness is my goal, and I am inspired to do one hundred crunches instead of fifty lunges, then I'm going to do one hundred crunches. This might be because deep down I care more about a flat stomach and strong core than buns of steel. Leaning in to what you truly care about taps into a deeper pool of inner strength and commitment.

If your subconscious mind (inner voice) knows that you don't care about a flat stomach, buns of steel, having the energy to run around – or any other area of benefit to your fitness goal – then it will be a struggle every step of the way, if you are able to succeed at all.

On the other hand, if your subconscious mind knows that you do value playing with your kids, having a strong core or toned thighs, etc., then you don't really need motivation. You will be inspired on all levels and it will show!

When I work a problem down to the real truth, it may be ugly but it is motivating because I find the inspiration necessary to make the changes that are important to me. Motivation is like a spark that ignites our dreams; inspiration is like the Olympic flame burning eternally and being shared worldwide.

The bottom line here is this: a great life is not about what you say you want, or even about what think you want. Instead, it's about what you are willing to show up for and do for yourself. Believing that you deserve it, and having a mindset geared for success, are the first steps in creating the results that you desire.

Old Goal: Get up at 5:30am and workout for an hour.

New Goal: Workout daily to support overall fitness and health so that I can enjoy activities with my family.

Old Mindset: "I want to be in swim suit shape for summer" The meaning this gives my subconscious is that I am going to work hard and sacrifice for a goal that is only enjoyed a short time.

New Mindset: "I want to feel good in my clothes and have the energy for the activities I enjoy." The meaning this gives my subconscious is that I care about my fitness and forever enjoy the benefits of good health.

Exercise:

When you're given the safety instructions in the preflight briefing, there is a reason that they have you put on your own oxygen mask first... If you're dead, you'll not be able to help *ANYONE*! This includes the people who you love so much that you keep *putting their needs ahead of your own.*

1. Identify an area in your life in which you're not putting yourself first and ask yourself, "Why?"

2. What message do you send to yourself... or what is the voice inside your head saying to you?

3. What would you gain if you did put yourself first?

4. What do you give up because you are not taking care of yourself first?

5. Identify one small thing that you could start doing today that would greatly improve your life if you continued to consistently do it.

(Extra Credit: If there are other areas where you do this, repeat the exercise with each of them.)

Are you in your own way or are you supporting yourself to get to your goals?

Which step have **YOU** reached today?

Chapter 2
Sometimes It's Just A Bucket

Life can be so incredibly exciting, can't it? The chances are that when you read that sentence, it brought an image to your mind that was positive, fun, and thrilling. Maybe it was of a fun day at Disneyland, or of a day at a county or state fair, or taking a fast drive on an open stretch of highway with no other cars in sight. However, there are two sides to the coin of excitement... one is positive; the other is negative. While one way to see excitement is through the lens of an exhilarating experience, another is through the excitement of something that terrifies you beyond belief. What this shows is something that I wholeheartedly believe; it's all about perspective.

Many top athletes describe their feelings just before a big competition with the same words that someone else would use to describe the most terrifying moment of their life. Among such feelings are: feeling butterflies in your stomach, the rush of adrenaline, a sudden clarity or euphoria, or the feeling of time either slowing down or speeding up. While all of these feelings could be attributed to great excitement and joy, they could also apply to a sudden sense of fear and massive dread.

If we spend our lives living in a worst-case scenario, then it can be difficult to see and remember the times when things turned out better for you than you thought they could... maybe even better than you could've ever imagined!

When we have no discipline of the mind – always allowing our thoughts to run wild – we usually tend to allow our imaginations to come up with some crazy, and often dramatic, outcomes.

I was driving home from work one day, on a busy main road at around 6 o'clock on a week night, when I saw someone on the side of the road who looked like they needed help. There was already one other car with a couple in it, who'd pulled over to help. Seeing this, I was assuming that all that was needed was to push it to safety onto the shoulder of the road. I drove a little past the group and pulled into the next neighborhood so I wouldn't leave my car in the way and cause more issues.

After I parked, turned on my hazard lights, and ran back to the broken-down car, I realized that this was not such a simple issue. The couple who had already stopped were talking to the girl who owned the car (a 2018-ish, Dodge Challenger) about what had happened.

The guy in this couple seemed to have a decent handle on some of the basic issues to check for, and ask her about, as he tried to help. He'd checked all the easy stuff... that the steering wheel wasn't locked up, the emergency brake wasn't on, there were no flat tires, etc. And while the girl driving the Challenger was also running through what had happened, *none of it made sense as to why the car would suddenly stop*. She said that all of a sudden, the wheels locked up and began to make a terrible noise if she tried to move at all, so she pulled over. As she tried to go forward, the screeching and scraping noises that it made were awful... the type of grinding, scraping noise that made her immediately think of the number of zeros that would be on the repair bill.

As all of this was happening cars were zooming by, without giving us a safe or comfortable amount of space. This prompted me to use the flashlight on my phone and stand behind the car so that I could wave the oncoming traffic into the next lane, something that was less than ideal, but necessary. A police officer stopped by and asked if it was an accident. Seeing him there, I was hoping to get some traffic control support from him, but unfortunately he was responding to another call. Promising to send someone our way, he was gone as fast as he had arrived.

At this point, I was doing my best to come up with some other solutions besides us figuring this out *on the side of the road*. Nothing seemed to work. Then the guy helping out jumped in the driver seat and decided to give it a try. If you ignored the *horrific* noise it made, the car moved forward in a mostly normal fashion. Upon hearing this noise, I could definitely understand why its sudden onset made her pull over. However, since the danger on the road was high, and the car was able to move, we did the smarter thing by getting it safely into an adjoining neighborhood.

Once we were out of traffic, we all took a look under the car to try and solve this riddle.

Low and behold it was nothing more than <u>*a bucket*</u> that was lodged under the car... and a bucket that seemed to have just a little bit of paint left in it.

"Yay for random sh*t on the road!"

We tried to kick it out from under the car but unfortunately that was a dirty waste of effort. Luckily, she had some golf clubs in the trunk, and using one of them we were finally able to whack it to the side and out from underneath her car. She was so incredibly relieved that the car she loved would not need tons of expensive repairs.

While I was glad to find out that the issue was so simple, I also found myself frustrated that we hadn't thought to look under the car sooner. I realized that my acceptance of other peoples assessment effected my own set of choices. If I'd been willing to look at the problem with fresh eyes, then maybe we could have avoided most of the frustration, not to mention the danger of standing in traffic. What if I had seen the bucket instead of directing traffic? We might have solved the problem faster. Someone also could have been hit by a car. Things could have gone better, or they could have gone worse. Either way, the point is that now that it's over, all I can do is decide what I learned from the experience that I had and carry that lesson forward.

Once when I was living on my own in this cute little two-story townhouse in Tempe, Arizona, I happened to experience one of the scariest moments of my adult life. It had begun as an average day for me, and one without even the hint of doom or gloom in the air. I was upstairs taking a shower to get ready for a date that evening. Since my hair was already done, I had a shower cap on and just needed a quick rinse and shave to feel glamorous for the dinner I was anticipating. As I started to scrub-a-dub-dub, I suddenly heard the most terrifying noise ever!!

The funny thing was that every time I stuck my head outside of the shower curtain, *I heard nothing*. But moments later, with my head back under the water, *I'd hear it again.*

Suddenly I started to run through the terrifying list of possible scenarios that this could be, almost certain that there would be an assailant running up my stairs at any moment with the most sinister of plans in mind for me. With this sudden rush of thoughts running through my mind, I knew that I had to come up with a plan of attack for this most-assured impending doom!

In that moment I realized that there's something so vulnerable about being nude in the shower. Then I thought that maybe I could to use the 'naked factor' to my advantage, perhaps surprising the attacker. In a split second, I'd decided that if a figure came through the door, I would lunge at them with the shower curtain and try to wrap them up in it like a straitjacket. Then this brought up the mental imagery of either running outside naked, or of first stopping for a robe or some other clothing. Then I realized that my doing this would give the intruder a second chance to get me, so 'negative' on grabbing a robe... naked it would be.

Well after a few seconds that felt like several hours – running through both the terror and my attack plan – I finally realized what I was hearing… it was *the sound of the water hitting my shower cap!*

Seriously?

The emotional trauma that I'd endured because of something so simple and obvious was astounding to me. In moments like these I do enjoy reflecting on what my response was and where my mind goes in a moment of terror. On the other hand, maybe a few deep breaths, accompanied by a little more rational thinking, just might have saved me from that energy-draining adrenaline rush.

Such encounters as these can either strengthen us, or chip away at our inner power. If, instead, I had lived in the, "Yeah, it was a shower cap *this time*," mindset, then I could have let this derail my whole living situation. Such a thought process could have brought about the decision that this neighborhood is a little scary and that living alone was more dangerous than I'd originally thought. Maybe I should *worry a bit more* and invest in a security system to make sure that this fear never comes true. Instead, I laughed at myself, told a funny story about it, and moved forward. In fact, I was a little empowered by the strategies that I'd devised if it *had* been an intruder.

No doubt about it, our thoughts can run wild. If we aren't careful about where we allow them to go, we can end up lost in the woods of the world. Being intentional with life, and knowing what you want to get out of it, is important for taming such wild thoughts. In a way it's like being a kid who's afraid of monsters. You may have to check under the bed for a while, but eventually you empower yourself with the knowledge that they just aren't there. Shadows can cause doubt, but with the light of day you can see more clearly that those monsters were everyday objects that you were simply seeing from a different perspective.

As a kid of about five, living in Iowa, I had a terrifying clock in my closet. Worse yet, my bedroom was on the top floor of a *creaky* three-story house. On any night that I'd forgotten to close my closet door before my mom put me to bed, the street light outside would reflect on the face of this Mickey Mouse clock, and when it did the eyes looked demonic. Crossing the bedroom to close the door meant braving anything that could be lurking under the bed. Doing my best to silently slink across the cold, creaking wood floor didn't help because of my fear that my steps might awaken something even scarier.

From this situation, I learned the value of habit. Remembering to close that closet door was crucial to my 5-year-old sanity and serenity! However, at that age habits are not always easy to form. Eventually I realized that I had to summon the inner strength to overcome my fear. When I finally did, I could go to sleep peacefully... with or without Mickey glaring at me.

What I've found about myself is that I, 1) like to make things difficult on myself, and that, 2) I like a challenge. Instead of having to remember to shut the door or learn to be strong, I could have just asked my mom to move the dang thing. There are always many solutions to a problem or multiple answers to a question. The ones we pick are decided by either our filters or our perspective.

Sometimes in life the scariest thing that we're facing is *our own wild imagination.* While there is real danger in the world, a lot of the time it's nothing more than just a bucket, a shower cap, or a creepy clock.

"Fear is not real. The only place that fear can exist is in our thoughts of the future. It is a product of our imagination, causing us to fear things that do not at present and may not ever exist. Do not misunderstand me danger is very real, but fear is a choice."

- Will Smith

At the first sign of trouble, in what life situation(s) do you imagine the worst taking place?

In the instances in which everything works out, do you truly acknowledge that particular win and the better outcome? I find that sometimes I continue to look at those situations from a place of "I'm so glad it wasn't as terrible as I thought! I thought it could have been this, that, or even something else."

Let me tell you that the mindset of, "It wasn't as terrible as I thought" is not where you want your mind to live. Assuming the worst, and thinking terrible things anytime something goes wrong, *is a practice*... and a destructive one at that. It's also one that does not serve you well or get you closer to your goals. The thoughts we dwell on are more powerful than a momentary thought of relief.

In the case of the car, she could have pulled safely into the neighborhood and assessed the issue. But because of a sound that triggered her own inner fear response, her brain caused her to freeze in place. It's important to listen to what the surrounding world is telling us; it's also important to pause long enough to make intelligent decisions.

Exercises:

Bring to mind a time that you thought a problem was bigger than it was. Describe your reaction to that problem and what was not productive about that for you.

What was the actual outcome or solution?

When you think back on that time now, do you remember what you thought would happen, or do you remember what actually happened?

If you are still running the "but what if... would have happened" model through your head, spend one to two minutes remembering the relief that you felt when it all worked out. Focus on the details and get specific.

Chapter 3

Don't Let Relation Ruin Relationships

Enough said.

But is it?

Your life is *your* choice... and more than just DNA.

Sometimes we put all of this love and effort into people who aren't good for us *simply because we're related to them.* To be honest with you, sometimes these people are GREAT! Yet at other times, they're not. Realize one important detail of life:

This isn't your only family.

We have both a family of *origin* and a family of *choice.*

With that said, it's important for you to choose the people you love; the ones who bring out the best in you. Remember that these are not always the people who go easy on you. In fact, it's usually those people that you want to avoid when you've behaved poorly. Yet, the people who show up for you are the ones you want to invest in. You're best served to *invest* your time, money, and effort into the people who enrich your life, even if they're not always easy on you. People who expect nothing of you and don't hold you accountable, might not be the ones who care most about you. While it may be easy to be around them, they are not the ones who bring out your best self.

Some of my favorite parts of our family are those people who are not technically our "blood relation." When we met at 14, my best friend Jo and I looked like identical twins. We used to argue with people who thought *for sure* that we were at least related. Eventually we learned that it was a lot easier to say, "Yes, we're sisters." Just like so many others in my life, Jo is a wonderful part of my family by choice.

Then there are relatives... people you're related to by either blood, marriage, or adoption. We're so grateful that our families are filled with amazing people who we love. However, on my mom's side the only surviving relatives are people who she never wants us to meet. Then again, on Brandon's side there's an uncle that no one really ever sees or speaks to. For some people the percentage of unhealthy relatives is much higher than for others. Those who aren't on speaking terms with one or more members of their family are in higher numbers than most would think. (Isn't family supposed to be the most important thing?)

If you are fortunate enough to have people in your life who you love, and those who love you, adopt them into your family and treat them as such! Life is both short and beautiful, as well as long and tough. Family makes it a whole lot more fun. Don't get hung up on technicalities. Love is both the best gift and also the best bond. When you love someone, you find it hard to let them go, no matter what stupid things they've said or done.

Family is worth being a good friend to. Communication is the key to love... there is *no greater accomplishment* than true *love.*

Please, make no mistake in reading this. When I say this, I don't mean romantic love; I mean truly loving and accepting someone for who they are. Sometimes, that type of love doesn't come easy... often requiring lots of effort. Yet in the end, it's worth it. When was the last time you that had something *really* worth having that you didn't have to *work* for? I rest my case.

Family and friends are worth the time that it takes to nurture each relationship. While there are days when it doesn't feel that way, and you "just can't," there are all of the other days that more than make up for them.

So just what is family? Let's take a few moments to look at a formal definition of the word, then I'll expand on that a bit.

Family (n.)

early 15c., "servants of a household," from Latin *familia* "family servants, domestics collectively, the servants in a household," thus also "members of a household, the estate, property; the household, including relatives and servants."

Such a definition sheds light to a focus of *serving*, or being of service to yourself and your family, then seeing where that takes you. If you're choosing an amazing set of people whom you feel that you deserve to have in your life, then you will find amazing results in serving them. By the same token, if you're serving people who do not serve you, then you will find hurt, loss, frustration, anxiety, exhaustion, chaos, struggle, and more.

If you're feeling the side effects of toxic relationships, then maybe it's time to look at those who you're calling family.

To help you hone in on this subject for yourself, ask yourself the following questions:

Who are you willing to serve?

Who are you willing to love?

Who are you willing to help?

Who are you willing to care for?

Are those you feel this way about the kind of individuals who are willing to do the same for you?

Where have your choices led you in the matter of family?

Are you satisfied with your choices and their results?

Exercise:

Name someone currently in your life who you allow to treat you in an unhealthy or disrespectful manner. (Write their name down in your notebook, then answer the following questions about them.)

What is your relationship with them?

Why do you allow the behavior or treatment that you're allowing from them?

Is there a boundary that you could set or a change, that would impact that relationship in a positive way?

Could you improve any relationship in your life by both individuals simply agreeing to disagree on a specific 'thorny' subject? If so, is it possible for both of you to do so?

Chapter 4

No Tools Necessary

At this point you know that Brandon is my husband... he's also very handy. In this chapter I'm going to talk with you about really knowing your partner. What motivates them? What does NOT motivate them? And... how to ask them something of a challenging or sensitive, personal nature (or maybe even something as simple as a complicated favor) in a way that creates a win-win for both of you.

When my husband and I bought our first house, there were a few projects that we did before moving in. One of the biggest projects that we took on was renovating the laundry room... to me, the configuration was all wrong! I was definitely the one who wanted to change it around so that it had a better workflow. To be honest with you, I am not a great lover of doing laundry, and I'm even less enthused when I feel that the space set aside for that activity sucks in its layout. One bright spot in this situation is that the house didn't come with a washer and dryer, so the room was already pretty empty.

One day as Brandon was headed to Home Depot for some more supplies, he left me with a task. Handing me the BIG sledge hammer, he said, "Just take out everything you don't want."

'Simple enough', I thought, and since demo has always been one of my favorite parts of any reno project, I hoped that he meant what he'd said as he walked out the door.

Once he returned from his run, he found that I had the room down to the studs on the bottom half, and was now working on the many layers of flooring that I'd discovered in the process. All totaled, we ended up having to remove *five layers of flooring* before we could lay the new tile that we'd bought.

To begin, there was a layer of thin and cracking tiles. Under that we found a layer of linoleum... then more linoleum... and just for good measure, yet *another* round of linoleum. Layers three and four were the worst because there was nothing but yucky glue on both sides of the crumbling squares. By the time of his return, I'd made it through all of the layers in about half of the room. The double-sided layer of gooey, sticky, and broken, sharp linoleum eventually became the overall buzzkill to my initially-energized motivation.

Thankfully for both of our sanities, Brandon was willing to step in and finish the job. He moved all the laundry hook ups, re-tiled the floor, and painted it to match the new red washer and dryer that we'd just purchased. (In all reality, he had to work *very hard* to get me those appliances, but that's a story for another day.)

Anyway, the laundry room reno came out beautifully, and, to say the least, I was thrilled with the results! After moving in, we threw ourselves a house warming party to finally have all of our friends and family over for both some good food and an evening of fun (as well as showing off the fruits of our recent labors).

One thing about Brandon and I is that we *love* games! We have card games, board games, yard games, video games, and *tons* of sports gear for whatever mood tends to strike our fancy. This was a great party, and to our pleasant surprise, there were even some great gifts... one of which was a gift card for Bed Bath & Beyond. Yay for us, since there were still a few items on our list of 'must haves' for the house; one in particular that I had in mind for this gift card.

The one thing that both Brandon and I really wanted was a wall-mounted soap dispenser for the master bathroom shower to clean up the clutter of shampoo, conditioner, body scrub, and various other bottles that cluttered up our shower floor. Since we're big believers in saving water, so much the better to shower together... thus, all of these bottles on the floor had become a very significant problem.

I was excited to spend some of our gift money, so armed with my list of items, I headed off to Bed Bath & Beyond. I'm sure that I spent over an hour looking at all kinds of things that were not on the list, however, I did eventually get around to the items that I'd written down. I was very pleased to find they had a couple of options in the brushed finish that we wanted for this particular item. After a lot of comparison shopping, I finally picked a nice 3-piece dispenser and continued to hunt for the trash can that I felt I could live with for the foreseeable future.

When I got home, I couldn't wait to show Brandon all of the fun things that I'd bought for our house! To my great pleasure, he *loved* the soap dispenser that I'd chosen... and because of that I felt like a *winner*. I left it on the dining room table so he could mount it to the shower wall in his 'spare' time.

This was my *first* mistake.

Days, then weeks, went by. Finally, after week two, I thought to myself, 'Maybe he just doesn't think about it when he's out here in the dining room.' So, in order to help prompt him with this particular task, I took it into the bathroom and set it on the cabinet where he would have to see it.

More days went by.

At this point, the site of that stupid box began to incite rage in my mind. I kept thinking to myself, "Why doesn't he just put it up? He's done much tougher projects in the last few weeks! WTF!?"

One day while I was in the bathroom, I happened to notice a little picture on the box. It was one of those international symbols; a circle about one inch in diameter, inside it was a picture of a hammer and a screwdriver with an 'X' through them. Next to this little circle, for anyone who still didn't get it, were the words, "No tools necessary". Then it clicked.

Suddenly I realized that Brandon *loves* to build, make, and fix things. With something so simple, I was now convinced that he didn't care about putting up this soap thingy with double-sided tape. In that moment I looked back at all of the frustration that I'd caused myself over such a simple matter. I'd been assuming that since he was the handy one, that he should be putting this up... and every day that he *didn't*, my frustration grew even more.

With my sudden realization, I literally started to laugh out loud because it was so simple. To be honest with you, I *love* these easy projects. So I grabbed a cotton ball with some alcohol on it, cleaned the surface of the shower wall where I wanted to mount it, opened up that bad boy, and slapped it on the wall *in less than five minutes*. I love simple tasks like this because I can check them right off my list in no time flat.

Put up the soap dispenser. Check!

This happened at a time that was early in our relationship, and fortunately I had already learned a couple of these lessons. However, this is still one of my favorites because of how quickly it clicked once I got it.

> *"The most important thing in communication is hearing what isn't said."*
>
> - Peter Drucker

Since then about 8 years have passed. As I was starting to write this book, I talked to Brandon about some of the stories that I wanted to share in it. This particular story was one of them, which surprisingly enough brought up a great discussion about the whole situation. Once I shared my memories of this story to him, he thought that all of my dramatic frustration was hilarious. Simply enough in his mind, it all boiled down to one simple point... "I had never asked him to put it up."

My jaw dropped. Not only was that true, but *there was more.*

"What if I had put it in the wrong place?" he asked.

"If you would have put tape on the wall where you wanted it, I would have put it up. But God forbid that I put it in the wrong place."

I didn't even know what to say to that. Suddenly a thought came to me. 'Would it really have been so scary to 'mis-place' the dispenser on the shower wall?'

Yes! The answer to that one is most definitely yes.

I'm sure that at *that time in life* I would have thought it was a *huge deal* for something to *not to turn out the way that I'd planned it.*

To really and fully know your partner takes time, effort, and a desire to understand them. Fortunately for us, Brandon and I both have a deep desire to know and understand each other. It's such a practice shared between us that keeps us on this journey with one another. Many of our friends say that we're lucky... that we have an awesome relationship. However, what most of them fail to realize is that we both *work very hard* on our own growth, both as individuals and our growth together as a couple. Doing this requires constant practice along with a dedication to our future together.

After the soap dispenser incident, I learned some valuable lessons that I strive daily to put into play. Next up – a few months or maybe even a year after that lesson was learned – I had yet another growth opportunity. WooHoo!

At one point, Brandon was a heavy equipment operator. As part of his safety gear for this job he had to wear heavy, steel-toed boots. However, one incredibly annoying aspect of this is that he would take these boots off and leave them *in the middle of the kitchen floor*. Tell me this... who in the world takes their shoes off in the kitchen anyway? My point is this... these shoes happened to be a bit hidden from normal view and as a result, presented a danger at times when walking through the kitchen.

To this day the reasons behind such a behavior remain a mystery to me. I, on the other hand, *love* to walk around our house barefoot. On way too many occasions I've walked into these shoes *in my bare feet*. These include:

- Stumbling into them late one night when all I needed was to get some water before bed.
- Coming home with groceries and not seeing over the top of what I was carrying and tripping over them (and nearly falling).
- There was even the day when I caught a boot with my pinky and ripped the nail off. (I'll not mention here the incredible pain that accompanies such an event. Oops... I just did. Never mind.)

I was so upset about this particular incident that I'd had enough; I plotted my revenge. I waited for a later time to 'trip' over his shoes and throw the blame at him *when he least expected it.*

If you want an amazing, loving, respectful, and meaningful relationship, *this is not the tactic that breeds success.* In time, I finally realized that it would take me less time to put his shoes where I wanted them than it would to plan and launch a plot against him. Instead of harboring anger and discontent, I started to look at how fortunate I was that we were together. From there, I just decided that anytime I found them, I'd just *move them*. As a result of such a simple choice, I was happy that his shoes were where I wanted them to be, instead of them being *right in the way*!

Since Brandon likes things to be put away 'in their place', he appreciated me for doing this. That doesn't mean that he would start taking them off and putting them away himself. It simply means that he appreciated my doing it. I also appreciated that he didn't care *where* I put his shoes, and other things, as long as I would shout him an answer about where something was if and when he'd ask me from the other side of the house.

Quick question: What is it about going into another room that makes you want to talk to the person who you'd just been next to a few seconds earlier?

While it may seem easy to throw blame at someone else, when I began to look at the energy wasted by doing so, it was actually much easier to silently, or even, on occasion, grumblingly, take action. Actively choosing what I will give my time and mental energy to can be very empowering. By working to conquer my own frustrations, I help myself build a greater sense of self-esteem and self-worth. What's even more delightful is that by releasing that energy and moving the shoes cheerfully, eventually he started doing so as well.

There are still times when I might shout or complain and it's important to feel those moments... you know, let it out and let it go. Holding on to frustration is one of the most destructive choices that anyone can make. Doing so will affect your health, your self-esteem, your relationships, and steal your energy from being able to more fully experience some of the exciting parts of life.

Is that frustration, or that 'inconvenience', really worth your own peace of mind? If so, what you're saying is that whatever that *thing* is, it's more important than either you or your relationship with the person to whom you're throwing blame.

Re-read that last paragraph. As you do, think about where you might be letting this happen in your own life.

Exercise:

What is something small that someone else does that "just drives you nuts," that you could easily take over in yourself or change?

What would happen if you took action instead of living in the head space it takes to blame someone and be upset?

What would you do with all of that free space in your mind if you let go of all of these little resentments?

Chapter 5

Sometimes the Same Way IS Different

My husband, Brandon, and I can do the same thing but come out with completely different results. Why? Because sometimes the same thing is different. Allow me to explain.

Most things in life involve such a variety of factors that you have to *know* that the outcome will be *different nearly every time*. Two different people doing the same thing will inherently bring their own biases, decision making processes, and for lack of better term, style, to the way something is done. Following are a couple of examples.

First Example

Brandon and I used to work within two miles of each other in approximately the same area of town. While I worked at a co-work/event space, he was working at a manufacturing facility making AC units for large industrial applications like tech company server rooms and military facilities. We both drove to work Monday through Friday, leaving from our house in the morning and returning home at night. However, we took very different routes to work. There would be days that I would either get into a *mood*, or miss a light, which would prompt the sudden thought, "I'm going to go his way today!" From there everything would go horribly wrong, and as a result, now I'd be running late. With this, I'd not only be frustrated with both the traffic, as well as being late to work... worse yet, I'd ALSO *blame him*. The conversation in my head would go something like this: "Why did I listen to him? This is so stupid! I should have trusted *myself* and gone *my way*!!"

While at times that would be the end of it, most of the time I'd find a reason to bring it up later and make a comment to him, in real life, about my morning issues by going *his way*. I'd do it in a manner something like this:

Brandon: "Hi babe, how was your day?"

Me: "Well it was great, except I tried *your* way to work today and got totally screwed up, so I ended up being late. Because of that, I wasn't ready for my meeting and as a result, I then spent the whole day playing catch up!"

How many times do we make decisions based on someone else's judgments or choices, and then hold that person accountable when they weren't even a part of what took place?

Here's the truth of the matter. The *same route* to work, taken at a different time of day (and driven by a different person), is going to *be* a *different route*. He would leave for work at 5:30 in the morning to be at work before 6:00. His route had three school zones that had no restrictions or traffic during that time. When I took the same route at 7:30 on the very same morning, I'd hit every school zone and usually ended up behind a couple of slow-moving school buses. (Grrrr....) My experience was often one of being trapped behind a bus that had to stop for a minivan, then finally getting past it, just to be stopped by a crossing guard. His experience, quite unlike mine, was that it was the most direct route with the least number of traffic lights to slow him down.

I hate to admit the number of "fine, I'll take his way" days that I had before realizing how different it was, just because of the time of day. It was something so simple. Since, in our relationship, he is the one who is better at directions, as a result of knowing this I usually defer to him. Therefore, when I'm having a tough day with my choice of route (compounded by the stress of the situation), I now start to think that maybe somehow his way will magically be different. However, when it's not it's somehow *his fault* and *he has let me down.*

When we go camping and are hiking in the woods, make no mistake, *he* is the one you want to *follow back to camp.* We even play a game in which we walk random directions away from camp. Then I pick the direction that I think the camp is from where we are, and he picks the direction that he thinks it is, and *then we see who's right.* (Spoiler Alert: He *always* wins this game.) This is why I trust him implicitly when it comes to directions.

However, when he isn't with me and I choose something because I *thought* that's how he would do it, that is not the same thing. I like to hold him accountable for my results but that's more than a bit unfair. This is kind of like having a dream in which someone does something really messed up to you, but then after you wake up, you're mad at them in real life.

Second Example

Another time that this type of miss-association caused a serious conflict in a close relationship of mine was with my best friend when we were about 14 years old. She had danced for most of her childhood and performed many times. As a result, she was well versed in stage makeup and had a kaboodle* full of it.

> (*Kaboodle: If you don't know what this is, it's a container with many trays and drawers for all of your makeup and various accessories... somewhat similar to a tackle box, or tool box.)

There was a particular red lipstick with top coat that she assured me would be a commitment of at least three days if I wanted to put it on. However, based on my own experience with lipstick, I had an issue getting lipstick to last on me for any length of time whatsoever. In fact, it's usually gone in ten to twenty minutes... *no matter how careful I am*. Being that we were both teenagers, we heatedly debated this topic, taking it nearly to the point of meltdown before deciding to just test the theory. We both put on the lipstick. *We were both right.*

Hers did not come off *for three days*. Mine was gone *in twenty minutes*.

To this day we're still friends and look back on this story as such a good lesson in our friendship. (More about the lessons that I've learned about friendship in Chapter 8. Don't worry... we'll get there.)

There are times when we take things so far before realizing that the information that we're basing the argument on is different. If your starting ground is different, but you follow the same directions, you will most definitely end up in a different location. The worst thing you can do is fight with the person who would be on their way to find you if you weren't arguing about their directions being wrong.

Activity: Remember to take time for fun! Part of personal growth and learning is knowing when to take a break and have some fun. This is your reminder to pause today and everyday for something that makes you smile. Doing something that brings you joy is a great way to get re-energized.

Which way should the toilet paper go? Ahh... that old chestnut.

Well, there are many answers and many reasons. My story starts back before my husband and I were married. It was about 13 years ago that we were dating and staying over at each other's houses. As we spent more and more time together, different things would come up.

One of the most ridiculous arguments happened to arise from the toilet paper roll. To be honest, the way in which you re-stock the toilet paper actually matters when you have other people in your house. This can be true for siblings, roommates, and spouses. We both had an opinion about it... and of course they were very different.

I happened to think that the roll should go with the flap towards the back. The best description I have EVER heard concerning this topic is the following:

You either like "The Mullet" (flap in the back) or "The Beard" (flap in the front).

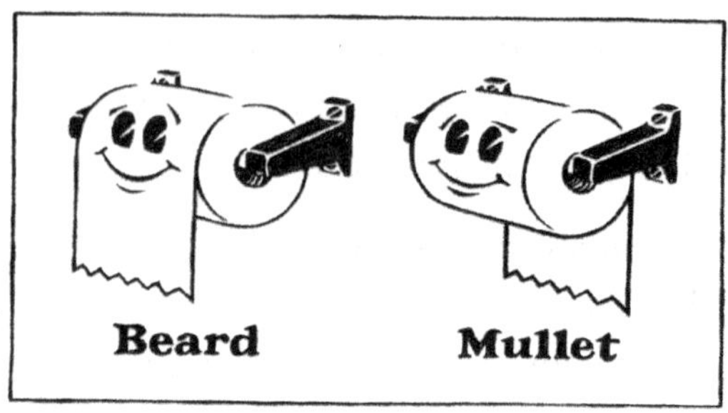

I like to use the mullet method while he prefers the beard. We definitely argued about this, making whatever arguments one can make about toilet paper. (Growth opportunity – It's TP!! Be glad that someone had the decency to refill it and *move on with your life*. If it bothers you that much, replace it the way that you prefer and see if anything is mentioned. If not, hooray!)

After many years of love and growth, I've conceded that I don't really care about this one way or the other, and I'm happy to replace the toilet paper whichever way that he prefers. I truly appreciate having a partner who helps out with the day-to-day tasks that keep our house running. Appreciating the help he gives, instead of criticizing it, has been a much more effective way to continue getting his help. Being flexible about how something gets done, as long as the overall outcome is positive, will free up time and space in the relationship. This principle is a big part of leadership. Delegation is much more effective when you trust your team to get it done. However, when you delegate, release the reins on exactly how it's done as long as the agreed upon outcome is the same. At home or out in the world, your team can be both your greatest asset and most valuable teacher.

It's important for you to be honest about the things that you care about in your relationship. Finding a middle ground on the important things that you have differences about is important. Yet, just as important, if not more so, is to not to worry about the issues that you care little or nothing about, one way or the other.

I can't express how much I don't care which way the roll of toilet paper goes, *as long as it's there.*

Now, over a decade later, I was struck with the exact reason that I chose the mullet method over the beard to begin with!

Our cat, one that was mine from before we were together, is 15 years old and is now up to some of her original kitten shenanigans once again. As a kitten, one thing that she *loved* to do was to perch herself on the toilet lid and scratch at the toilet paper roll until it was *all* unrolled on the floor. The other day, she did that *exact* thing again... and then I remembered why I put the toilet paper on the roll with the flap in the back. When it's a 'mullet', her scratching does not unravel the roll the way she likes it, so she gets bored... it's not worth her time. However, if you put the beard out there, she just *loves* to see how long it takes her to unroll the TP.

We now agree on the mullet method.

Keep in mind - Our experience of an event is processed through our own specific mental filters (along with past experiences) that we associate with that specific current event. It's these filters that significantly impact the way that such information is received.

TIP: For small, silly, or no longer provable instances, we suggest the following time-tested strategy. If you really care about the relationship, and your collective desired outcome is for a better relationship – as opposed to someone being right or wrong – you can use even and odd days to easily decide who 'wins' (actually, it's not a win, but who realizes their desired outcome) on any given day. 'Who's right' can come down to, 'Well, who's day is it?'. I prefer even numbers, so in my life I'm 'evens' and Brandon is 'odds'. Again, this is *only* used to solve minor disagreements.

Here's a way to apply this principle. A guy runs by wearing a hoodie. I think it's blue, my husband thinks it's green. The man was there and gone, so now there's no chance to look again.

Brandon: "I like that green hoodie he's wearing."

Me: "You mean that blue one, yeah it looked good."

Brandon: "No that was green, just like my green hoodie that you also think is blue."

Me: "Well if you mean blue like that blue hoodie that you think is green then yes, it's the same. Lol. Okay who's day is it?"

Brandon: "Well today's the 9th, so I guess I'm right."

Me: "Yep, you are right, that was an awesome green hoodie!"

Here is the real key to using this tool. You have to mean it! The next chapter goes deeper into this topic, but it's crucial here, too. When we settle a squabble applying the even or odd days method, it's because neither of us wants to argue... instead, we just want a satisfying outcome. Being able to win or lose and move on is important to us and we think it's a fun way to give us an out on something that many would see as nothing but stupid. If one person constantly uses this on their days, then it's not being used in good faith. It's because of this that such an intentionally playful technique will not be of any service to your relationship if you abuse it.

Exercise:

Think of a disagreement you've had with someone important in your life, in which at some point, you realized you were both talking about different things but you did not handle it well.

Write out the scenario and what both parties were aware of or discussing.

You:

Them:

Now explain how you would have liked to handle that situation or conversation differently.

What other possible outcomes do you think there could have been?

Chapter 6

Sure, I Learned That Lesson

There are moments in my life when I say to myself, "Damn, how did I manage to do *this* again?" On the other hand, I also find myself saying a variation on that theme with the words, "How in the hell did I do this again when I even *knew better not* to do it!"

Some things are silly and not of big enough consequence to thoroughly commit to. For me, I spill coffee pretty much every day that I have it, which is every day. Now it's finally turned into a kind of game that I play with the Universe. I try not to spill my coffee and yet I find new and even interesting ways of constantly doing it. Sometimes I overfill the cup. Other times I forget that it's in my hand and bend down to grab something (usually my phone that I've dropped), and there it goes again.

On the more interesting days (when I manage to slop coffee all over my car because I set it in the cup holder too aggressively and when I do it shoots everywhere like a volcano), I also miss the drinking hole in the lid and pour it all down my front, or oddly enough, any other place that it finds to go. Let's just say that the Universe *does not discriminate* concerning the various places on which I can spill my coffee.

I've become so desensitized to it by now that unless it's a spill of an epic level, it's not even a blip on my radar for that particular day. Instead, it's just a slight nuisance that I briefly acknowledge, then move on from there.

However, there are other examples of lessons that *I thought I'd learned* that can have a much bigger impact on my day, or week, or month, or even your year. How many times have I had a hangover and thought – when even the simple *thought* of another drink makes me gag – "I'm *never* drinking again."

'Miraculously', after a little time passes and I start to 'feel better', I then suddenly begin to think, "Yeah, a cold beer *does* sound good."

How many losers have you dated (or watched a friend date) and thought, "Are they ever going to get it together?"

It's human to put our blinders on for things that we either don't want to work on or even think about. Sometimes we know better and do it anyway... just because it's fun. This definitely applies to the dating world. In some areas, when it doesn't seem like there would be any real benefit to making such choices and actions, it often begs the question, "*why do I keep repeating this over and over again?*"

"Regrets should be a lesson learned, NOT a lifetime of misery."
- Jesus Apolinaris

Working in an industry that I hated, or for people who I didn't respect, was definitely something that I had to do a few times before finally figuring it out. While the opportunities to work for these types of people still come up, I have finally learned to say a big ole "Nope" to any of those 'opportunities' that still occasionally come along. As I continue to hone these skills, I am able to decline the offer much sooner as I identify the first warning signs.

Here are some of those red flags:

- I go into a business meeting with a person, or team, and it's clear that they don't truly mean the things that they're saying.
- Their body language doesn't match their words.
- A lot of 'trendy' or 'hype' words are being thrown around in the conversation.
- Promises are being made to me that have a lot of nice words, yet they don't define any clear expectations or compensation. "...and of course, we want to make sure that you're taken care of. You're a crucial part of the team and you should be rewarded." This is when the phrase, "shoulda, coulda, woulda" comes to mind.
- Most of all, when everything that's being said either sounds rehearsed, or agreed upon before the meeting (like a story that's been told over and over again), and it's difficult for you to get deeper questions answered.

The definition of insanity is doing the same thing over and over again, but expecting different results. While I have my moments to the contrary, I don't want to *practice* insanity. Being an active learner and listener in my life has helped reduce the time that it takes for me to learn my lessons. Once it's been learned, I have to care about the consequences (and not suffering them any longer) in order to commit it to its practice.

Exercise:

What are the top three lessons that life continues to present to you, that if you fully learned them, doing so would completely change your life?

1)

2)

3)

What have you been gaining by not learning those lessons?

Chapter 7

Say Things That You Mean AND Mean Them!

If Brandon is out in the yard working on a project and I come out and say, "Is there anything I can do to help?" I really mean *anything*. If he says "Yeah, I'd love a beer..." or a sandwich, or whatever the case may be, am I prepared to say, "Yes dear, coming right up!" and mean it? Am I going to do it with love and joy in my heart? Or... is there a chance that I will do it while thinking of a snarky comment to somehow fit into our conversation?

After years of being committed to meaning what we say to each other, I can honestly say that we happily do whatever the other person is asking. When the goal is to help, whatever that looks like is not up for judgment. When we did renovation projects there would be times where 'helping' was literally standing behind him with a pile of screws in my hand, being ready to hand him the next one, and the next one, until the job was done. This is also a silent task. Being the human screw dispenser does not include asking questions, checking my phone, or doing anything other than being ready to hand him that next screw.

If the help someone asks of you feels beneath you, this tells you that there's a definite opportunity for growth and learning. I allowed those tasks to teach me things like Mr. Miyagi would teach 'Daniel-san' in the movie *The Karate Kid.* Being quiet, watching my husband work, and trying to anticipate the next need, gave me insight into how he does things and in what areas I can provide support. This is true, and also adaptable, into other areas of life.

When my goal is to wholeheartedly support someone, whatever that looks like to them, then my commitment is to do what is asked of me, and not what I assume.

Have you ever been talking with a friend who is telling you all about a problem they're in the middle of (whether it's about home, or work, their love life... it doesn't matter), and the whole time you're thinking to yourself, "Easy, I've got this. I know *exactly* what they need to do!" Yet when you start to offer your solutions to 'fix' their problem, you find out that the problem you *thought* they were explaining was actually very different.

Say, for example, I have a friend who is going on and on about how bad her job is... not making enough money, terrible boss, all of the typical complaints about work. I start thinking things like:

"Who do I know that's hiring?"

"Where could she find better pay and better management?"

As I start to offer solutions and bring up the companies that I know are looking for people, she begins to get defensive and tells me that I don't understand. As we dive deeper into her situation, it turns out that she's not making enough because she's either not getting the hours in or shifts that she wants, and these are the things that are causing the issue with her manager. I was trying to solve the problem based on what I *thought* it was and how I would handle it. Yet, all that I needed to do was listen to and support her. Once she's said what she needs to say, all I need to do is show her that I know she has everything that she needs to handle this problem for herself in the way that best fits her values.

Most of us want to be heard and validated by someone who cares about us. If we have ideas about solutions then we want support for them, but otherwise we don't really want someone to try to *fix* the situation for us.

"It's not at all hard to understand a person; it's only hard to listen without bias."
- Criss Jami

When I come home and tell my husband about an issue at work (or something that happened with my car), he jumps in to help by asking a bunch of questions and trying to take immediate action. *Very rarely is this what I'm looking for.* I used to get so frustrated when he would start asking questions! I didn't want him to dig deeper. I just wanted him to let me complain and sit in the pile of emotional mud that I was temporarily wallowing in. I wanted him to know I was capable and willing to fix my own issue, *just not in that moment.* Instead, it was in that moment that

I wanted *my person to hear me*, tell me that it sucks... and then maybe offer me some chocolate.

When we were about a year into dating, he did something that has forever stuck with me. It's a story that I've told numerous times when talking to someone about "how I knew he was the one." One day I was really sad about losing a dear friend, something that had happened a few months before. This friend was young, and his end was quite tragic, so there was still a lot of hurt around that subject for me.

As Brandon was working on dinner, I was taking a shower. After I was in the bathroom for over half an hour, and the water had been off a long time, he first knocked, then peaked his head inside the door. Here he found me sitting on the floor in a towel, bent over the tub, sobbing. Mind you, this wasn't a soft, silent cry either, but the true dictionary definition of an *ugly cry*. Immediately upon seeing me in such a place, he quickly shut the door and disappeared. I thought that was absolutely the right move. I didn't want to be seen and I clearly wasn't ready to come out.

A few minutes later he came back with some water, a glass of wine, a chocolate bar, and some tissues. Without a *word*, he respectfully cracked open the door, slid them inside near me, then just as silently closed it, giving me the space that he could tell that I needed. In that moment I felt such a sense of relief that he knew me well enough to know that I didn't want to talk or be hugged... yet. In cases like this, I like to work through my feelings and then get hugs once I'm on the other side.

*Hugging someone in these moments of such dramatic hurt and pain can actually anchor that feeling to the sensation of the hug.

When he handled that situation so perfectly, and without any input from me, that was when I first felt a sense of deep comfort thinking about our future together.

Exercise:

If you are struggling with a problem in your life? How can the people who love you, support you best?

1)

2)

3)

What actions or words do you find to be the least supportive?

1)

2)

3)

Who in your life do you feel supports you best and why?

Chapter 8
Just Help Me Set My Expectations

I've encountered this particular aspect of life a lot, especially in dealing with businesses. Whether it's a business-to-business interaction, or one of business to consumer, it's a real challenge to have one consistent set of expectations because every company has very different policies and practices.

For instance, when calling in on a customer service line, the automated systems tend answer your call in one of two different variations.

One way of answering your call is in a manner that does its best to make you feel important (while making you feel as though they're *doing you a favor*), as in, "Your call is very important to us, please continue to hold."

On the other hand, the other way of picking up your call is more exacting so that you don't feel as though you'll be on the phone until hell nearly freezes over, as in, "Your estimated hold time is (however many) minutes, please continue to hold."

If you have a certain set of expectations when going into any situation, then you could be setting yourself up for unnecessary frustration and anger.

Yet, while setting your expectations can be difficult, it's also incredibly crucial for all manner of relationships.

We have a friend, we'll call him Todd, who is incredibly challenged at being on time for things that we've planned. For that matter, he's challenged to even remember that we've made plans. This is not because he doesn't care or doesn't want to hang out with us, but it's just *his own way of managing his life*. At this point in the friendship, we've learned some very effective techniques to apply when making and keeping plans with Todd. The most basic is to call him about an hour before we're supposed to get together. Since he's usually napping, this seems to be enough time for him to wake up, get himself ready, and make it to our house *on time*.

As I said, we've been friends for a *long* time. Through the years, he's set our expectations of who he is and what his interests are. As a result of this, we're now able to plan and operate accordingly. What makes this all worthwhile is that Todd's *a lot of fun*... and there are definitely game nights, paint nights, or various other events that we really want him to be a part of. When we want him to come to something, we know what will be required of us for the event's overall success.

We'll make plans in advance, make sure that he wants to come, remind him as it gets closer, call him an hour early, and be okay if he's running a little late. We do all this from a place of love and friendship without getting upset or offended *because* we've had the conversations, set the expectations, and agreed on being okay with the outcome. Todd also doesn't get mad that we don't invite him to everything all the time. He just wants to be himself, run his life in his own way, and not have his friends (as well as others who are in his life), try to push him to order his life differently.

> *"You are your own worst enemy. If you can learn to stop expecting impossible perfection, in yourself and others, you may find the happiness that has always eluded you."*
>
> \- Lisa Kleypas

However, we have other friends who have some of these same struggles. Yet, instead of being accommodating, they aren't willing to admit this (especially to themselves), and work to find somewhat reasonable solutions to a particular challenge. Those are the friends we've stopped inviting to the various fun events that we host in our home.

I remember one particular weekend that we were having a party. While I can't recall now if it was my birthday or Brandon's, I do remember that it was a party with a purpose. For this one we'd also invited a bunch of friends from all of our different groups. One of the girlfriend's I'd invited had been texting me throughout the day, asking what she should wear, what I suggest she bring... you know, the typical questions someone who's excited to come to a party would ask.

Towards the late afternoon she now asked me if she could bring a friend with her because they had another party to make it to after ours. Since the policy at our house is, 'the more, the merrier', I told her that we were equally excited to have her friend be part of the evening.

However, as things got under way, I stopped getting any texts from her... in fact, once the party was in full swing mode, I'd yet to hear anything from her. Finally, I texted her and... crickets. (Okay... let me be clear here, she didn't text me the sound of crickets. What I was trying to say was that I heard nothing at all from her... whatsoever.)

I couldn't believe that something like this would happen with her, especially after all of the years of friendship that we'd shared with one another. However, that's the way that things ended... and we haven't invited her to another of our parties since.

It is absolutely okay to change plans with someone. However, it is also absolutely crucial to communicate any changes – especially last-minute ones – with them if you care about the relationship. Communicating changes helps everyone manage their expectations of one another... again, something very crucial to aid in maintaining a valued relationship.

Anger often begins to creep into our emotions because of unmet expectations.

There have been plenty of times when I've had to either change or cancel plans. For me, the most important aspect of this is that *the moment* I know that there will be an issue (whether a delay or a change) with the plan, *I communicate that with the others involved.*

As well, there have been times when I've wished for more time to be ready for a dinner or a party with friends. On the other hand, when someone tells me, "Hey, I'm running 15 minutes late," it's usually that little extra bit of time that I've needed. (Isn't it funny how things tend to work out like that?) Yet, there are other times when such changes provide crucial information, especially if it effects cooking times so that I'll have food hot and ready when our guests arrive. While on occasion, such last-minute changes can be quite inconvenient, it's always better to know than to be left in the dark.

For example, if you're an hour drive away from your planned location, but leave with only fifteen minutes to get there, you know that you'll be late. If that's the case, then let the other person know immediately. That communication should be honest and accurate.

"I just left so I'm about forty-five minutes away."

Please do not shrink away from the truth and say something like:

"I'm running a little late, but I'm on my way."

This not only is a lie that tries to avoid responsibility; it still doesn't communicate an accurate time for the person on the other end. One step up from that communication would have been to let that person know forty-five minutes sooner since you clearly didn't leave on time.

"I am running late; I plan to leave in ten to fifteen minutes. I'll confirm with you as soon as I'm on the road, but it looks like I will be about forty-five minutes late."

This type of communication lets the other person know you are aware of your commitment, that you're taking responsibility for your lateness before they're even aware of it, and it gives both parties time to re-negotiate the plans if necessary.

My general rule of thumb for being on time is to allow and extra ten minutes for every hour of travel. If I have a five-hour drive ahead of me, I plan to leave about one hour before I need to in order to allow for traffic delays, additional pit stops, and any other potential source of delay.

Another not-so-wonderful side effect that results from a lack of communication is that it gives you time to write a scary, crazy, angry novel in your own head about what it is that's causing the delay; one that's filled with your own set of reasons, issues, and scenarios. If someone who is usually reliable is running late, but fails to communicate this to me, I can so easily begin to create all sorts of terrible scenes in my mind. However, if I know that they're just running late, then I can easily carry on until the time they last communicated to me, without a single concern.

Setting your own realistic expectations of yourself and others is one of the simplest methods that's available to set yourself up for success.

Exercise:

Come up with at least one example of this in your life and write it down.

List the benefits that you're getting from this.

List the prices that you're paying as a result of this particular incident.

What action could you take to improve that scenario?

Are you willing to take that action immediately?

❑ Yes

❑ No

❑ Not Now (If not now, then when?)

Chapter 9

Why is it called "Making Friends"?

Both Brandon and I were raised by parents who moved around a lot throughout our childhoods. As a result of some of the unique skillsets that we've gained from such an upbringing, we've built a strong bond with one another. Don't get me wrong here, there are also negatives (you know, the bad with the good), and those stories are for another day. However, the important takeaway from this is that time after time, we're both able to start fresh over and over again.

When I've had to start again in yet another new place – meeting people, making friends, learning the lay of the land, and becoming a part of a new community – doing so many times over has built certain skills. When mentioning community, that can apply to many different things – a whole town or city, a school, a job, and also a new hobby or activity. There were also times when I was starting over that it felt like it was more than a bit difficult... having to establish all new bonds and connections with people can be a lot of work.

On the other hand, it can also be AMAZING!

Have you ever felt stuck?

Have you ever thought about how much you've changed, while no one seems to have noticed?

Have you ever wondered how different you could be if you simply had the space to grow?

When you start over, you get to set new expectations, establish new sets of boundaries – along with new sets of dynamics – with the new people in your life. (Too many 'new's in that sentence for you? If you experienced great stability growing up, then just pause here for a moment and imagine every first day of school being in a new city and how many 'new' circumstances that might bring along with it.) However, in all of this newness, there is still something to be wary of and pay attention to, which is the fact that whenever you 'start over', you're still bringing 'yourself' (meaning whomever it is that you are) along for the ride. If you're generally a miserable person who hates everything in your life, changing your location or scenery will *not* make much of a change for you over the longer term.

On the other hand, as you learn and grow there will be times when getting a fresh start will help shift your momentum in a more constructive, positive direction. Understand something very important here: You don't have to move to another state, or even a different city, for this to happen. Sometimes it's as simple as finding a hobby that you've not yet pursued, then meeting a group of people with a similar interest that you didn't previously know.

Getting to practice your new skills, while cultivating a more refreshing outlook, and/or changing the way that you make decisions (or whatever it happens to be that you're working on), can help make these inner changes become habits that are easier for you to maintain, especially when you're around people who know the old version of you.

> *"We meet the people we're supposed to when the time is just right."*
> - Alyson Noel

So, back to the point at hand. Why is it called "making friends"? Because in a real way you do have to make friends with those who come into your life. If you're new to a community, you have to volunteer something of yourself in order to be incorporated into their established social structure. Accomplishing this can be as simple as introducing yourself around to others, as well as showing an interest in what everyone has going on. However, there are times when the process can be much more complicated than what I've outlined above.

In my late teens and early twenties, I found it difficult to make male friends because their girlfriends would feel threatened by me, even though *I had no intentions of anything romantic with their man*. This was true whether he was a boyfriend, husband, or significant other. However, it's hard for someone to trust that about anyone at first meeting, because *trust is something that's most often earned*.

It wasn't long before I learned that if my intention was pure, then the best way to accomplish this goal was to *first make friends with the wife or girlfriend!* If we were all meeting at a party, and a male friend of mine happened to bring his girlfriend or significant other for the first time, I would *ignore him while getting to know her*. To begin, I'd find something simple that I liked about her then compliment her about it. Having broken the ice with her, I'd then spend time getting to know her, then mention some of the great things that her guy had already told me about her.

Again, you must have pure intentions for such an approach, otherwise you're being deceitful and people pick up on that, even if it's subconscious in nature. If I want to be able to hang out with my friends, not cause trouble in their life, and possibly even make another new friend, this strategy is one that's been received quite well overall. On the other hand, if you don't genuinely like someone and just use these tactics to act like you do, then using this technique is something that everyone will easily see through.

But seriously... making friends can be *hard*. There are so many factors involved in the process. First of all, it helps a lot if you have something in common with the other person. Then the two of you need to be somewhere reasonably close to one another on a consistent basis making it easier, and more enjoyable, to get together. Finally, you have to put effort into getting to know another human being.

There are times when you'll make an effortless connection with someone, have a great time with one another, both like each other, and *it still doesn't stick.* How does this happen? It's simple... life.

I have had amazing friends who I absolutely loved, but due to a change of location it was a friendship that was no longer worth the effort to maintain. I used to spend my summers in a state away from the one I lived in, make a bunch of new friends, then leave and return to my home, in a place far from where I'd spent my summer, to go back to school. Once I was home, I'd make friends again. Yet, come summertime, I'd leave for the season. Due to the considerable distance involved, a life like this made it incredibly tough to keep up relationships... especially between the ages of five and fifteen.

Worse yet, this was at a time before cell phones.

Needless to say, during these years of my life if you had a telephone in your room, that was a *huge* deal. This was also a time in life, the tween and teen years, when kids would change so much that you could leave for the summer as friends, then return in early fall for school to find out that you're suddenly enemies. (WTF was that all about?) A few of those summer breaks made big differences in kid's lives and the groups they became a part of. Since I wasn't around to pick a group, I'd come home thinking that somehow life would be the same. Yet, to my surprise (and baffled disappointment), it wasn't.

One time in particular, this happened when someone new had moved from a bigger city into my town. We'll call her Tess. While she was this tiny girl, Tess had somehow become the queen bee of my social circle. She and her younger sister, Angel (who was quite the opposite of her name) basically became my nemesis.

These were the days of jump rope and tetherball. In jump rope, Tess would skip turns to spin the ropes and cut in on other kid's turns... doing a great job of playing the bully.

I never liked someone like that, so I'd fight back; jumping in on her turns or stop spinning the ropes when she jumped in. Since she was such a bully, I thought my friends would back me up and be happy that someone had finally stood up to her and told her "No." Instead, I got the opposite. People I'd been close with the previous school year suddenly decided that *I* was the one in the wrong because *they wanted her approval.*

This form of behavior shows up in adult life, too. I've stood up for friends who came to me with a problem, only to have them back down and change their story. As a result, I ended up being the bad guy. I've said it in previous chapters, but I'll say it here again... it is very important to choose the people who you feel are worthy of your time. This is not a stuck-up attitude, but one of knowing your own value and worth, then sticking to it. I have also learned that if the person with the problem is not the leader in the solution, then any efforts to help on my part can end up either wasted, or worse... hurtful.

As an adult, such behavior can be most evident in the work place. You may have a team that works well together. While everyone in the current team knows and respects each other, when someone new comes in it changes the entire dynamic of the team.

If you're a strong team with a clear vision, this can be nothing more than a speed bump for the team to overcome. Yet, if you're a group that is barely staying motivated and already spinning around the drain of decency, then such a change can be crippling.

I have found team work to be one of the most effective forces in the world. When you have a group of people who are backing the same vision, sharing a will to win no matter what the obstacles are, you can do incredible things together.

I've had the opportunity to lead teams of people that had never met, and had also never met me, who spent countless days doing thankless work in an effort to serve their community. While there were days with no wi-fi, missing supplies, staff shortages, and very little planning or notice, my team would always show up and do an amazing job. Other leaders praised our ability to succeed while other teams were floundering, and us asked how we did it.

The results I was able to achieve were rooted in the ability to quickly meet and connect with people. Learning what it takes to "make friends" – or learning how to present yourself in a vulnerable manner that makes people want to come along with you – is an invaluable skill for anyone to cultivate. The biggest secret is that you have to both want it and work for it. If it comes cheap and easy, then it probably is.

Those people who will pledge allegiance to you without a foundation are fair-weather friends. On the other hand, the people who will stick with you as you build a foundation together are the ones who are in it for the long haul. These are the ones who are worthy of your time.

It is important for you to be accountable to your friends, while at the same time holding them accountable. If someone slinks away from accountability, then it saves you time and disappointment… that time when you would have relied on them to do what they said they'd do.

Exercise:

List the people closest to you.

What is most important to you about those particular relationships?

What are you bringing to those relationships? How are you showing up?

Chapter 10

The James Bond Syndrome

At times I get so down on myself that I begin to think that I am nothing more than a terrible loser. Why do I suddenly feel this way?

Well, for one, I'm not as 'hot' as the hottest person I know (or see on TV).

I'm not as 'in shape' as the most fit person I've ever seen.

I'm not as 'smart' as the smartest person I know.

I'm not as 'good at soccer' as the person I know who's amazing at that sport. (David Beckham or Mia Hamm come to mind.)

I'm not as 'good at painting' as the best painter I know. (Bob Ross and those 'happy trees' that manifest on the canvas from out of a paint blur.)

While I could go on and on, I'll spare you for now.

I call this the "James Bond Syndrome." Why? While the character of James Bond has skills that any number of people could have, he is the *one person* who has *all* of them. There's an expert in one of these fields somewhere who might be able to overcome one of the many obstacles that he's constantly faced with (in the movies), but no one person has *all* of these skills at *that* level.

Comparing myself to others is like comparing *my real life* to other people's *social media portrayals of their life*. Social media is all about posting the things about your life that *you want people to see and hear*. If I only paid attention to the things that I did well in my life, then my self-talk would be incredibly positive *all of the time*. However, because I *know about my failures and shortcomings*, that positive talk takes a lot more effort for me to bring about. When I judge myself against any friends and family who have incredible skills in a specific area, I'm not only hurting myself, but I'm also hurting my relationship with that person. If I'm wasting energy being jealous or upset at myself for not being as accomplished as someone else, then I'm definitely not being supportive of, and excited for, them either.

I have genuinely given myself an internal thrashing because of how much more in shape some of my friends are than me. They spend hours at the gym and dedicate a major chunk of their time to building their muscles and increasing their fitness. However, I have to remember that I *choose to spend my time in other ways*. What on earth makes me think that I deserve to have what they have without doing the work that they do?

If there were a James Bond in real life, that person would have done *nothing* with their life but train and practice every moment of every day. If I really wanted to be so good at something that I was willing to do it all day, every day, then I'd be doing it.

I love my life. I love the experiences that I've had, and the people I've met along the way. Sometimes I learn something new and think, "Yeah, I want to spend more time doing this!" Take, for instance, painting. In the first place, it's not something I would have ever imagined that I would like as much as I do. My best friend, Jo, asked if I wanted to do a wine and paint night.

My reply: "You had me at wine!"

We had a blast and although we were there well after the class ended, I was pretty pleased with my work. After that, I went to Michael's Art Supply and bought supplies so that I could paint at home. Since then, the two of us have done a handful of our own paint nights with various friends. Overall, it's been an incredible experience for all involved!

On another occasion, without knowing what one another was doing, Brandon and I created two separate paintings that look as if they are one... and we're incredibly proud of what we've created. (Talk about being soulmates!) In fact, one of our paintings was used for the cover of this book.

Even better, even though they appear in black and white, I'm sharing both of them with you on the following two pages so that you can see how similar both of our paintings are to one another. I think that you'll be as pleasantly surprised as we were when you see them.

For the record, the above masterpiece is the one that I painted that night.

While on the other hand, the above painting is Brandon's work of art.

"The worst loneliness is to not be comfortable with yourself."
- Mark Twain

Those people who know me might think this is odd because I've done some wild things from time to time.

For one, I've gone sky diving a couple of times.

I enjoy cliff diving.

I've ridden off-road vehicles through incredible dunes at high speeds.

I can easily stand in front of a room full of people and talk to them without a script or any notes.

I put on events in which I cook for 20-60 people... and have also coordinated catering for 100+ guests.

I consider myself to be good at all of these things... but when I do something that I'm really good at, I don't give myself credit. Instead, I say things like:

"It wasn't really that hard," or...

"I didn't really do that much", or even crazier...

"It was no big deal."

These messages to myself do nothing to promote my own growth or excellence. Instead, they *zap the energy from me and reduce my ability to create amazing results.*

I'm learning that I've spent a lot of time ignoring the negative voice in my head, even pretending that it's not there (instead of giving it attention), and instead *choosing different thoughts*. However, when I ignore that voice it gets to keep running itself in the background.

When I realized this, I came to the decision that I'm done with allowing negativity and self-doubt to be my background noise. Instead, I've chosen to practice hearing the negative thought, saying to it "thanks for the feedback," and sending it on its way. By acknowledging the negative thought, and choosing to move forward with other more positive and enticing thoughts, I am very much amping up my own power!

Let me say that *one more time* just in case you scanned over it.

By *acknowledging* the negative thoughts and *choosing* new positive thoughts I have increased my power.

In many ways, it's like doing sit-ups. If you are just throwing your top half towards your bottom half and engaging as few muscles as possible (while still counting the repetitions), then you're cheating yourself out of the real workout. It takes far longer, if ever, to develop a toned core... especially if you're not engaging the right muscles.

That is essentially how I look at some of my previous techniques for developing better self-talk. Ignoring the negative talk was much easier than hearing it and choosing to think differently.

Another example would be trying to talk over that voice inside my head. When I layer a positive voice over that negative one, instead of just giving it a moment to be expressed fully, then what I'm doing is creating more noise in my head instead of changing what's being said.

This book is another chapter for me in my journey through life and self-discovery. In the months that I've been writing it, I've continued to learn from it with every re-read and conversation with those around me who are involved in the stories. As I share some of these chapters with close friends and family, I get to enjoy hearing what thoughts or impacts my stories have had for them. Feedback is not always pure joy, but as I give myself the grace to learn and grow without being immediately perfect, I definitely find the process more enjoyable.

During this past year, my husband has given me the most feedback, and because of this we have done the most growing together. It never ceases to amaze me how impactful our communication is when we're both coming from a desire to listen to, and be heard by, one another. At times it takes longer than we would like to be fully on the same page with what we're talking about. Taking the time to realize that we are talking about something, with very different ideas in each of our minds, actually saves a lot of time and frustration later.

In the first chapter I discussed the difference between simple and easy. In life, making a big change can be simple, such as, "just cut out carbs and sugars," while it's not necessarily easy. Learning tools and aligning your beliefs with what you want is simple. Yet, living out those changes can be quite the challenge.

When I changed my belief about my self-worth, and was inspired by the goal to love myself, I started to see where the real efforts come from in personal growth. It comes from the practice of those new beliefs and behaviors. It was simple for me to identify behaviors and responses that I wanted to change. It was even simple to learn techniques that allowed me to collect myself and choose a different thought or action. However, for me the *tough part* of change was the real-life application of that new behavior or response.

While I can make sure that my innermost desire is good communication and win-win outcomes, when I'm in the moment of frustration — even after I take a deep breath to pause — I still have to focus on and practice that new behavior. Until that practice becomes second nature for me, the 'simple' task of responding differently can still be quite difficult.

I had not spent enough time seeing what that new self-talk would sound or feel like. As a result, when a growth opportunity arose I was still stuck in the, "Okay, don't do what you usually do" mindset. The key to getting change to happen more quickly and effectively is to focus on the outcomes you *want to happen.* It's just like creating muscle memory for any other activity.

Think of a new baby learning to walk.

First, they hold on to things and wobble. (Learning the tools for making changes in your life and deciding what you want those changes to be.)

Then they walk with an unsteady gate. (Practicing new thoughts, feelings, and behaviors while seeing what works best for you.)

Finally they master the walk and start to run. (That *new* behavior first becomes *the* behavior, and then suddenly becomes that *old* behavior as you find ways to improve things even more.)

Remember what I said about learning a new skill. Once you learn it, the skill levels up and you start learning all over again.

It is my hope and desire that what you've been reading here helps you to learn these lessons faster and more effectively than I have. If this is the case for you, then I've fulfilled my purpose in writing this book... and we all win. By the way, if you've enjoyed reading this book, please share it with someone you love.

Exercises:

Have you ever experienced the James Bond Syndrome in your own life?

In which areas of your life tend to be those that you feel the least capable?

Do you think that you could ever come to the place in your life in which it's okay to be as you are without any improvements? In other words, do you believe that you could ever reach a place in your mindset in which you were willing and able to accept yourself just as you are without any additional changes or improvements? Write about this in your notebook.

Recap of Lessons:

Ch. 1 - Self Worth: Self esteem will energize all of your endeavors.

Ch. 2 - Fear & Imagination: Use your imagination to build your future and let go of the fear.

Ch. 3 - Relationships: Choose the ones that build you up not hold you down.

Ch. 4 - Communication: Sometimes it's not what you say, it's what you do.

Ch. 5 - Perspective: You can't always see all the variables but you can control how you respond to them.

Ch. 6 - Learning lessons: When you understand and connect the lesson it because part of you.

Ch. 7 - Listening: It's like meditations, you must quite your mind and hear with all your senses.

Ch. 8 - Expectations: Important to have, uphold, and be willing to change.

Ch. 9 - Relationships: Good or bad they take effort, nurture the good and let go of the bad.

Ch. 10 - Self Acceptance: We begin and end with ourselves. Choose to be someone you're proud of.

About the Author

Morgan's coaching journey started before she was out of high school. At first it wasn't about being a coach, but instead was about learning the tools and techniques that would aid her in transforming her own life.

Ever the entrepreneur, Morgan has spent the past two decades as an independent contractor doing everything from administrative work, to setting up new retail markets, and creating entire business divisions from scratch. She has managed teams of over a hundred people, and in doing so, motivated them to achieve incredibly unfathomable goals together. By the same token, she has also been someone who has helped small businesses run much more like well-polished corporations.

Morgan loves traveling the world and experiencing new cultures while finding ways to bring happiness to those around her. Her love for travel began before she was born and remains one of her driving passions to this day. In her travels, she's visited thirty states and six countries; most of them with her husband, and most recently with their dog, Benji, as well.

Realizing that the best results start at home, she has now turned her focus to one-on-one coaching. As a personal development coach and writer, Morgan is someone who is passionate about helping others live a life of joy, adventure, and transformation. Her mission is to help individuals find their true purpose in life, and in doing so, unlock their potential as they find and create a life that they love. To aid her in facilitating this goal, she has received training and certification in NLP (Neuro Linguistic Programming), Hypnotherapy, Time Regression Therapy, S.M.A.R.T. Goal Setting, Parts Integration, Reframing, and Anchoring to support incredible, and rapid change in her clients.

Now, as a coach and writer, Morgan is dedicated to using her skills to make the world a better place for everyone.

Coaching with Morgan

Twenty years ago, I started learning about personal development and some of the different tools people use to achieve their goals. In my first personal breakthrough session I remember telling my coach that "I don't want to be happy because happy people aren't as productive. Happiness is the goal of life so once you achieve it why would you keep working at anything?" That was genuinely my outlook on life because I had a lot of hurt and anger from childhood that I'd been carrying around. In order to not let all the negative emotions spill out, I had to hold back the positive ones as well. If I was willing to be really happy, I would also have to be in touch with how incredibly sad I was.

If you look up the definition of happiness you can find many answers. There is the Webster's definition, the Oxford definition, the Wikipedia definition, and so on. Dive further and you can get into the scientific study of happiness or the positive psychology meaning of happiness. When researching etymology (the study of the origin of words) you find that the word 'happiness" comes from words meaning either 'chance' or 'luck'. I believe that happiness means something different to everyone; what it looks like for me is not necessarily what it looks like for you. However, I also believe that everyone has an idea about what happiness means for them.

From my own personal experience, I began to realize that tackling any goal or problem that life would throw my way from a state of happiness – as opposed to a mindset of victimhood, complaining, and blame – netted much more successful results than any other mindset that I might choose.

When I said the words "Happiness Coach" to a friend of mine it was the scariest and most exciting thing I had said in a long time. The fact that it's not a well-known industry term or an established coaching style made my heart soar and my mind race. That jolt of excitement is one of the things I've learned to follow in order to be my most authentic self. From my experience, tackling any goal or problem life throws at me from a state of happiness is much more successful than any other mindset. This is my passion... helping others find their happiness and bring it home with them.

I believe if everyone treats themselves and others with love, kindness and respect most of the world's issues would resolve themselves. My vision is to bring more love and joy into this world by helping people find their happiness. If the style of my book resonates with you, and you are interested in having greater happiness in your life, **please email me for a consultation.**

Morgan Wolf
morganwolf.solutions@gmail.com

Suggested Additional Reading

Below is a short list of books that have helped me in my own journey of growth. I suggest you read if you would like to add more to your life in a positive way.

Think and Grow Rich - Napoleon Hill
7 Habits of Highly Successful People - Stephen Covey
Start With Why - Simon Sinek
The Alchemist - Paulo Coelho

All of rhese books are easy to find, whether on Amazon. com, or at your local bookstore.

Made in the USA
Middletown, DE
14 September 2023